Managing Editor
Mara Ellen Guckian

Editor in Chief
Karen J. Goldfluss, M.S. Ed.

Creative Director
Sarah M. Fournier

Cover Artist
Diem Pascarella

Art Coordinator
Renée Mc Elwee

Illustrator
Kelly McMahon

Imaging
James Edward Grace

Publisher
Mary D. Smith, M.S. Ed.

All About SUPER SENSATIONAL Me!

This Journal Belongs To

Author
Mara Ellen Guckian

TCR 8005

Teacher Created Resources
12621 Western Avenue
Garden Grove, CA 92841
www.teachercreated.com
ISBN: 978-1-4206-8005-8

© 2017 Teacher Created Resources
Made in U.S.A.

Teacher Created Resources

Hello!

You are unique. You are super-sensational! What are your interests? Your likes and dislikes? What about your dreams for the future? Use this journal to record your thoughts and sketch your ideas about all kinds of topics including you, your school, your adventures, and your favorite things. There are lists to check, ideas to circle, drawing spaces, and questions to make you think. You can draw or use the blank spaces to add photos. You can write dates, facts, and ideas and use your imagination to share daydreams and fantasies.

Take your time and be as descriptive as you can. You can skip around as a topic catches your interest and go back and add information as you have new experiences. Once you finish you will have a super-sensational journal all about you. It will be a great keepsake to read years from now. You will be able to see how you have changed as you have grown. You might be surprised and you will definitely enjoy reading about the many special times you've had.

Introducing... Super-sensational Me!

My whole name is _____.

I am usually called _____.

Today is _____ and I am _____ years old.

Here is a picture of me!

If I had named myself, I might have chosen the name

_____.

I like that name because

_____

_____.

The best thing about being my age

is _____

_____

_____.

When I Was Born...

I was born on _____
date

in _____ .
city   state   or country

When I was born I weighed _____ pounds _____ ounces.

I was _____ inches long.

I had _____ brothers and _____ sisters.

I was the   1st   2nd   3rd   4th   5th   or ☐ child in my family.

I was born in the

☐ **Winter**

☐ **Summer**

☐ **Spring**

☐ **Fall**

The best part of being a

baby might be _____

_____ .

Then and Now

I have heard stories about when I was a baby. I have checked all the words people used to describe me.

☐ active   ☐ fussy   ☐ silly

☐ cuddly   ☐ happy   ☐ sleepy

☐ cute   ☐ noisy   ☐ sweet

☐ funny   ☐ quiet   ☐ _____

My favorite story about when I was little is _____

_____

_____ .

Smart • Strong • Thoughtful • Athletic • Brave • Clever • Confident • Cooperative • Creative • Dependable • Energetic • Enthusiastic • Friendly • Funny • Happy • Hardworking • Helpful • Honest • Kind • Lovable • Organized • Outgoing • Polite • Quirky • Respectful • Shy

I have grown a lot since then! Here are three words I would use to describe myself now:

_____   _____

_____

How Tall Is Tall?

I have noticed that when people talk about babies, they talk about how *long* they are but when they talk about me, they talk about how *tall* I am.

I am _____ inches tall.

You could also say that I am _____ feet and _____ inches tall.

I am taller than _____.

I am shorter than _____.

When I grow up I think I will be _____ feet and _____ inches tall.

54 inches

2 inches

The best thing about being my size is that I can

_____

_____

_____.

17 inches

My Colors

Eyes

My eyes are

☐ blue   ☐ green

☐ brown   ☐ hazel

☐ I wear glasses.

☐ I don't wear glasses.

┌─ Here is my design for glasses. ─┐

Hair

My hair is

☐ black

☐ dark brown

☐ light brown

☐ dark blond

☐ light blond

☐ red

☐ other _____ .

My hair is ☐ curly ☐ wavy ☐ straight

I wear my hair ☐ the same way every day ☐ different ways

The Color of Me

My skin is ☐ dark ☐ medium ☐ light

☐ I have freckles. ☐ I do not have freckles.

My Family

My family includes many super people. I wrote some of their names in the quilt squares!

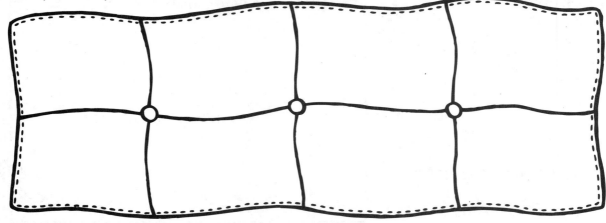

History

My family on my mom's side is from_____

_____.

My family on my dad's side is from _____

_____.

Tradition

One of our family traditions is_____

_____.

When I grow up, my tradition will be _____

_____

_____.

Super-sensational People

Some of my sensational people are not related to me. Let me introduce you to two more people that are special to me and tell you a little bit about them. I have added a picture of each of them.

_____

is special to me because

_____.

is special to me because

_____.

Home

This is a picture of my home.

I live with _____

_____ .

My favorite thing about my home is

_____

_____ .

My address is

_____

_____ .

I have lived here since I was _____ .

Before this house, I lived in

_____ .

We have _____ phone numbers.

Here they are!

_____

_____

Someday, I hope to have

a home that has _____

_____

_____

_____ .

My Best Memories

I have had some super-sensational days. Here is what I remember and why each memory means so much to me.

Memory 1

I remember

_____

_____ .

It was so *great* because

_____

_____ .

Memory 2

I remember

_____

_____ .

It was so *important* because

_____

_____ .

Memory 3

I remember

_____

_____

_____ .

It was so *special* because

_____

_____ .

My School

I go to _____ School.

I am in grade _____.

My teacher's name is _____.

My school is

☐ in a city.

☐ in a suburb.

☐ in a town.

☐ in my home.

☐ on an island.

☐ other _____.

To get to school, I

☐ walk.

☐ ride a bike.

☐ skateboard.

☐ take a bus.

☐ ride in a car/carpool.

☐ other _____.

Our mascot is a_____ .

It looks like this.

If I were the teacher for a day, I would _____

_____

_____

_____

_____.

School Is Important

My favorite part of the school day is _____.

👍 My favorite subject is _____.

I like to learn about something new by

☐ watching videos.

☐ memorizing facts.

☐ reading about it.

☐ trying it myself and practicing.

☐ using the computer.

☐ having it explained to me.

👎 My least favorite subject right now is _____

because _____.

I think I might like it more if I_____.

My favorite thing to do at recess is

_____.

Our school motto is

_____

_____

_____

_____.

I wish we could do

more_____

at school because

_____

_____.

My Friends and Classmates

I think having friends is important because _____

_____.

I try to be a good friend. One way I do this is by _____

_____.

When I am playing with one friend I like to _____

_____.

When I am with a group of classmates, we like to _____.

Some of my friends' and classmates' names are:

_____   _____   _____

I would try to welcome a new friend or classmate by

_____.

What It Means to Be a Friend

Here is a checklist of statements about friendship. I have circled **T** for True or **F** for False to show that I agree or disagree. Then I put check marks next to the three statements that are the most important to me.

T F Friends like doing things together.

T F Friends agree about everything.

T F Friends care about each other.

T F Friends are honest.

T F Friends never argue.

T F Friends help each other.

T F Friends share.

T F Friends try to be fair.

T F Friends respect each other's feelings.

T F Friends like all the same things.

T F Friends can say they are sorry when they need to.

T F Friends don't always agree, but they try to understand each other.

I think I am a good friend because I _____

_____ .

Best Day of School—So Far!

The best day of school so far was the day we _____

_____.

The best part of the best day was _____.

It was special to me because _____

_____.

This picture will help me remember the day.

If I could do one thing to improve my school it would be

_____.

I Am Happy When...

I like to feel happy. When I am happy I _____

_____ .

⭐⭐ Here are four things that make me happy:

⭐⭐ 1. _____

2. _____

⭐⭐ 3. _____

4. _____

Someone who makes me smile is

_____ .

Here is a picture of my smile.

I think the statement, "It is easier to smile than it is to frown" is

☐ True   ☐ False

because _____

_____ .

When I Am Sad...

The last time I was sad was because _____

_____ .

This was ☐ a big thing ☐ a little thing

To feel better I tried to _____

_____

Here are some other things I might try to feel better. I have checked the ones I think will work best for me and added some other ideas:

☐ Do something nice for someone else.

☐ Get some exercise.

☐ Talk about what is bothering me.

☐ Try to work it out.

☐ Say I am sorry if I did something I know I shouldn't have done.

☐ Other ideas_____

_____

_____

Mad, Mad, Mad!

Sometimes I get frustrated and sometimes I get really MAD. Here is my Mad Scale. I added little things that frustrate me and some more important things that make me mad.

Super Mad

Really Mad

Mad

Frustrated

The best thing I can do when I am really mad is

_____

_____ .

Scared—Fun or Not?

Being scared can be fun sometimes! Like when you are riding a roller coaster or when you go in a Haunted House.

For me, I think it is "fun-scary" when I_____

_____.

Then, there are times when I am scared (for real), like when_____

_____.

When I am scared like that, I try to_____

_____.

Other things I can try to do to be less scared:

⭐ Take 5 deep, calming breaths—sometimes more!

⭐ Talk about **what** scares me with someone important and try to figure out **why**.

What works best for me when I do not want to feel scared is to

_____.

I think it would be "fun-scary" to _____

_____.

I Am Grateful

To be grateful means to be appreciative and to be thankful. I know it is important to be grateful for the people and things that are important to me. Here are some words and pictures to show what I am grateful for.

I am grateful for _____.

I am grateful for _____.

Thank you!!!

Thank you!!!

I try to show that I am grateful by_____.

_____.

 #8005 All About Super-sensational Me!

I Am a Helper

I am growing up and can be helpful in many different ways. Here are just a few of the things that I can do.

At Home

_____
_____
_____

At School

_____
_____
_____

For My Friends

_____
_____
_____

For My Teammates

_____
_____
_____

My favorite way to be helpful is to _____

_____ .

I Can Give Back

I know that I am very lucky in many ways. I also know that it is important to give back to make our world a better place. I have checked some ways that I can help:

- [ ] Be kind to others.
- [ ] Don't litter.
- [ ] Donate books and toys.
- [ ] Donate used clothes.
- [ ] Help when it is needed.
- [ ] Plant a tree or garden.
- [ ] Recycle.
- [ ] Save water.

Each day this week I will do something special for someone and write it down.

Sunday _____

Monday _____

Tuesday _____

Wednesday _____

Thursday _____

Friday _____

Saturday _____

I am most proud of what I did on _____.

I Prefer...

There are so many things to do and sometimes I have to make choices. I have circled the choices I would make. Then I put a star next to four things I love to do or would love to try.

- **?** taking pictures **or** drawing pictures
- **?** building with blocks **or** doing puzzles
- **?** cleaning up parks **or** recycling
- **?** computer time **or** TV time
- **?** board games **or** computer games
- **?** ice-skating **or** roller-skating
- **?** making things **or** playing sports
- **?** skateboarding **or** bike riding
- **?** football **or** basketball
- **?** cooking **or** gardening
- **?** dancing **or** singing
- **?** drawing **or** painting
- **?** reading **or** writing
- **?** running **or** hiking
- **?** gymnastics **or** dance
- **?** soccer **or** swimming

Something that was not on the list of choices that I really enjoy is _____.

A Few of My Favorites

I am _____ years old and these are some of my favorite things:

App _____

Board Game _____

Book _____

Color _____

Computer Game _____

Fruit _____

Holiday _____

Indoor Activity _____

Outdoor Activity _____

Pet _____

Place To Go _____

Season _____

Time of Day _____

Vegetable _____

My absolute favorite thing to do right now

is _____.

One thing I do *not* like right now is:

_____

_____.

Animals—Yes or No

There are all kinds of animals in the world. I am going to draw or write my favorite in each group. I just might have to do some research!

Farm Animals	Forest Animals

Jungle Animals	Ocean Animals

Polar Animals	Desert Animals

Music

I have checked some kinds of music I listen to. In the musical notes I have written my current favorites.

- ☐ bluegrass
- ☐ classical
- ☐ country
- ☐ jazz
- ☐ my dad's music
- ☐ my mom's music
- ☐ pop
- ☐ rhythm & blues
- ☐ rock
- ☐ songs from when I was little
- ☐ other _____

Singers

Groups

Songs

I might like to be a

☐ musician   ☐ singer   ☐ songwriter

Right now, I play _____.

I think I might like to play _____ someday.

All Kinds of Books!

There are many types of books and many ways to read. I can read a book by myself or with a family member or classmate. I can read a book online or at the library.

For me, the best place to read is _____.

☐ I prefer holding books when I read.

☐ I prefer reading books online.

I have checked 3 (or more) of my favorite types of books.

☐ biographies

☐ fables

☐ fact books

☐ fantasy

☐ fiction

☐ folktales

☐ joke books

☐ mysteries

☐ myths

☐ nature and science

☐ nonfiction

☐ scary stories

☐ series books

☐ tall tales

I have written two of my favorite books below:

_____

_____

_____

My All-Time Favorite Books

FICTION

Title

NONFICTION

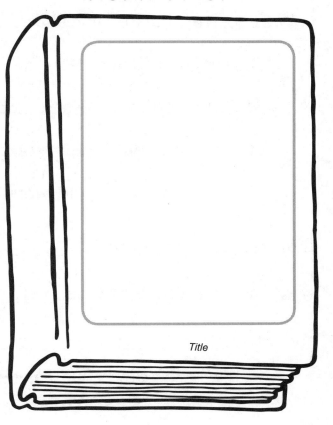

Title

I love this book because

_____

_____

_____ .

Main Characters

_____

_____

_____

This book is about

_____

_____

_____ .

I enjoy this book because

_____

_____

_____ .

TV and Movies

My favorite kinds of TV shows are

☐ adventure stories.

☐ fiction—stories that are made up.

☐ stories that have happy endings.

☐ stories that make me wonder.

☐ nonfiction—true stories.

☐ stories about animals.

☐ stories about machines.

☐ stories about space.

My favorite TV show is _____.

My favorite character is _____

because _____.

I loved the movie, _____.

It made me feel _____.

My favorite part was _____.

If I had the choice I might

☐ want to be an actor

☐ want to write the story

☐ want to direct the movie

☐ want to be a camera operator

because _____

_____.

I Am a Traveler

To travel means to go from one place to another. There are many different ways to travel. So far, I have traveled by

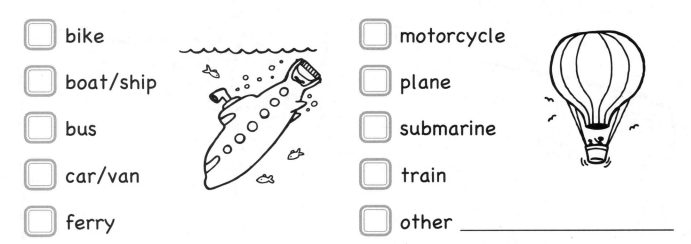

- ☐ bike
- ☐ boat/ship
- ☐ bus
- ☐ car/van
- ☐ ferry

- ☐ motorcycle
- ☐ plane
- ☐ submarine
- ☐ train
- ☐ other _____

My favorite way to travel so far is _____.

Someday, I would like to travel by _____.

I think it would be fun to travel this way because _____

_____

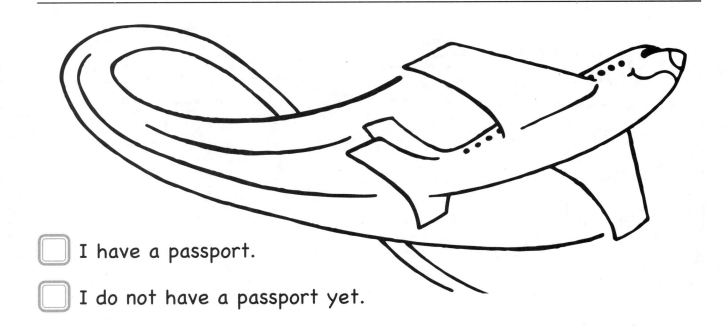

- ☐ I have a passport.
- ☐ I do not have a passport yet.

The Places I Have Been

People travel for different reasons—vacations, family visits, adventures, field trips, and holiday events. Here are some of the trips I have taken:

Things I brought:

_____

_____

_____

1. I went to _____.

I traveled by _____

The best part of this trip was

_____

_____.

2. I went to _____

I traveled by _____.

The best part of this trip was

_____

_____.

3. I went to _____.

I traveled by _____.

The best part of this trip was

_____

_____.

My Biggest Adventure

The most exciting trip I have ever taken was to _____

_____ when I was _____ years old.

I went with _____.

It was a

☐ day trip.

☐ family vacation.

☐ trip to visit family.

☐ "spur of the moment" idea.

We travelled by _____.

We saw _____

_____.

We got to _____

_____.

My Adventure Picture

States and Countries

There are 50 States in the United States of America. I colored in the states I have visited or lived in and added the abbreviations.

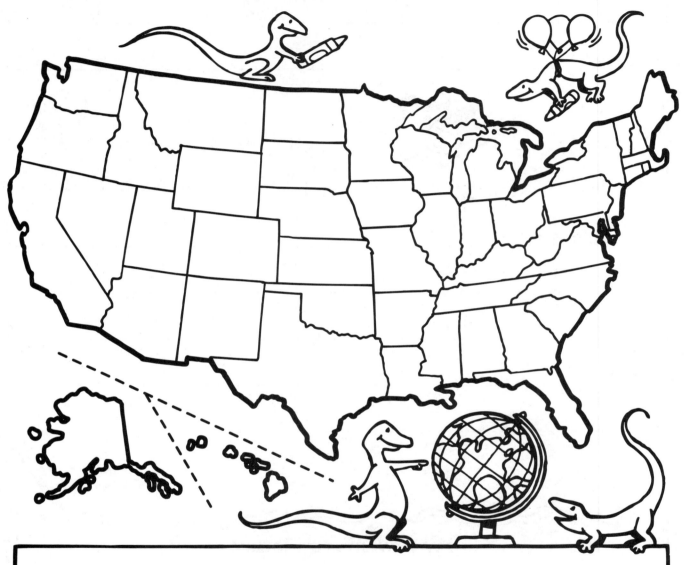

There are many countries in the world. I have visited or lived in

_____   _____

When you travel to different places you learn that_____

_____.

The Places I Could Go

Here are some places I would like to go and why!

First, I hope to go to _____

to see_____ .

While I am there I would like to _____

_____

_____ .

Second, I would like to go to _____

to see_____ .

While I am there I would like to_____ .

When I travel I like to bring these things.

Finally, it would be exciting to visit _____ .

While I am there I would like to_____

_____ .

My Perfect Day

It would be fun to be in charge of the weather, the food, and the location for a perfect day. The best part would be choosing the activities. My plan would go something like this:

Wake Up Time:

Weather for the Day:_____

Location: _____

What to Wear: _____

Event 1 _____

_____

_____

Event 2 _____

_____

_____

Event 3 _____

_____

_____

Extras!

_____

_____

_____

Food

_____

_____

_____

My perfect day would end at

When I Grow Up

I am lucky. I have time to try different things before I grow up and choose a career.

Some of the jobs people in my family have are:

_____   _____

I think my first job will be

_____ .

I can do this when I am _____ .
age

My First Job

When I grow up I might like to be a _____ .

I will need to learn to _____

_____ to be good at that kind of job.

The best part about this career is _____ .

_____ .

I might also like to be a _____

because I like to _____ .

For this job, I will need to learn to _____ .

If I Had a Restaurant...

My restaurant would be called _____.
My sign would look like this

I would serve my favorite foods. My menu would look like this

If I worked in a restaurant, I would want to be the

☐ Chef   ☐ Host   ☐ Taste Tester

☐ Dishwasher   ☐ Server   ☐ other _____

Magical Creatures

If I was able to spend the day with a magical creature it would be

- ☐ a dragon
- ☐ a fairy
- ☐ a leprechaun
- ☐ a mermaid
- ☐ a merman
- ☐ a troll
- ☐ a unicorn
- ☐ other _____

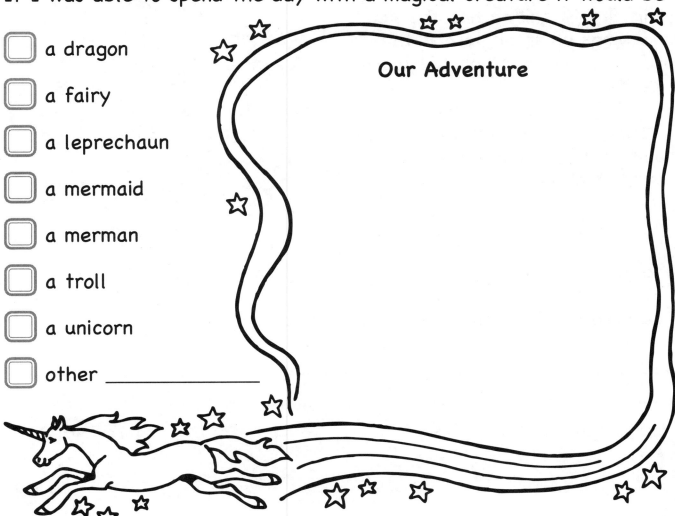

Our Adventure

I chose this creature because _____.

I think I might find this creature in _____.

We might spend the day _____

_____.

The best part would be _____

_____.

Combination Creature

There is a magical creature called a griffin. A **griffin** has the head and wings of an eagle and the body and tail of a lion. It looks like this ➡

If I made a creature that was a combination of two animals I would combine

a _____

and a _____.

The creature I created would be able to _____

_____.

It might look like this:

It would live in _____.

If...

If I could be in two places at once I would like to be in

_____

and _____ .

That way, I could _____

_____

_____ .

If I were invisible,

I would _____

_____

because _____

_____

_____ .

If my body was like a rubber band, I could

_____

so that I could

_____ .

I would look like this:

My Invention

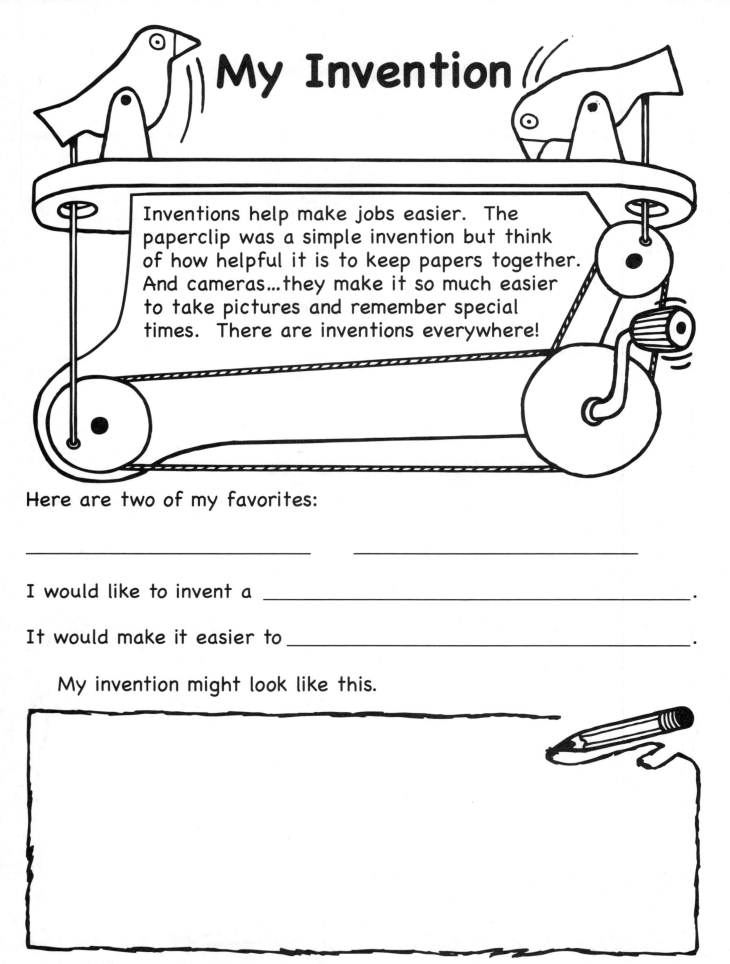

Inventions help make jobs easier. The paperclip was a simple invention but think of how helpful it is to keep papers together. And cameras...they make it so much easier to take pictures and remember special times. There are inventions everywhere!

Here are two of my favorites:

_____   _____

I would like to invent a _____.

It would make it easier to _____.

My invention might look like this.

Under the Sea...

If I could breathe under the sea I would have quite an adventure.
I have checked off some of the things I might like to do.

- ☐ find treasures
- ☐ frolic with fish in a coral reef
- ☐ live aboard a sunken pirate ship
- ☐ play with mermaids
- ☐ relax in a rocky crevice with an octopus
- ☐ spy on sharks
- ☐ wander with whales
- ☐ other _____

The adventure I would like to do first is _____

because _____.

I imagine I would _____

_____

_____.

If I could be any real sea creature I would be a

_____.

If I Had a Space Ship

If I had a spaceship it would look like this when it was flying.

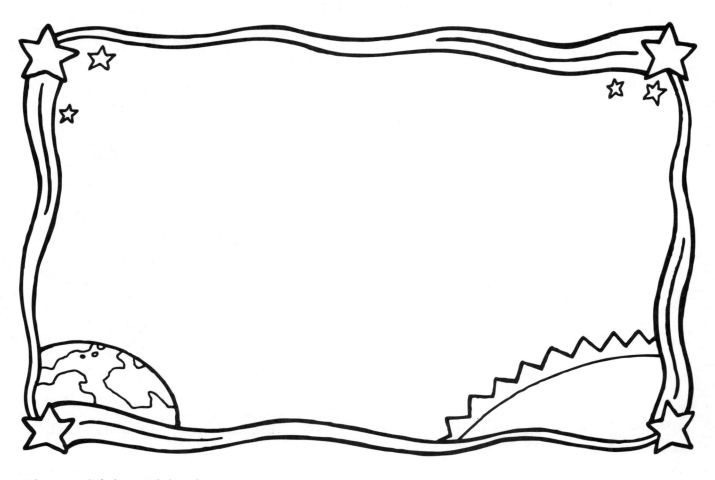

It would be able to_____.

It would hold _____ passengers. In the back there would be

room for _____.

I would travel to_____.

It would take _____to get there.

I would expect to see_____.

I would need special_____.

If I Lived in a Tree

My tree house might look like this.

I would use it as a

☐ place to go when I wanted to be alone.

☐ place to get together with my friends.

☐ both

To get to it I would need

_____.

If I were an animal living in this tree I would be a _____.

If I Were a Video Game

The title of the game would be _____.

There would be _____ important characters. Here are some of their names and what we would look like.

_____   _____   _____

I would be_____.

There would also be _____.

There would be _____ levels to pass.

To get to each level you would have to _____.

The goal would be to _____.

If I was in the video game looking out at people playing I might think that

_____.

If I Were a Superhero

My super name would be _____.

My super power would be _____.

My super costume would have _____

_____.

I would have a special symbol on my costume that looked like this.

The colors would be _____.

My super goal or quest would be to _____

_____.

If I *really* had my super power, I would use it to _____

_____.

Three Wishes to Share

It would be amazing to make dreams come true. I would make one for my family, one for myself, and one for the world.

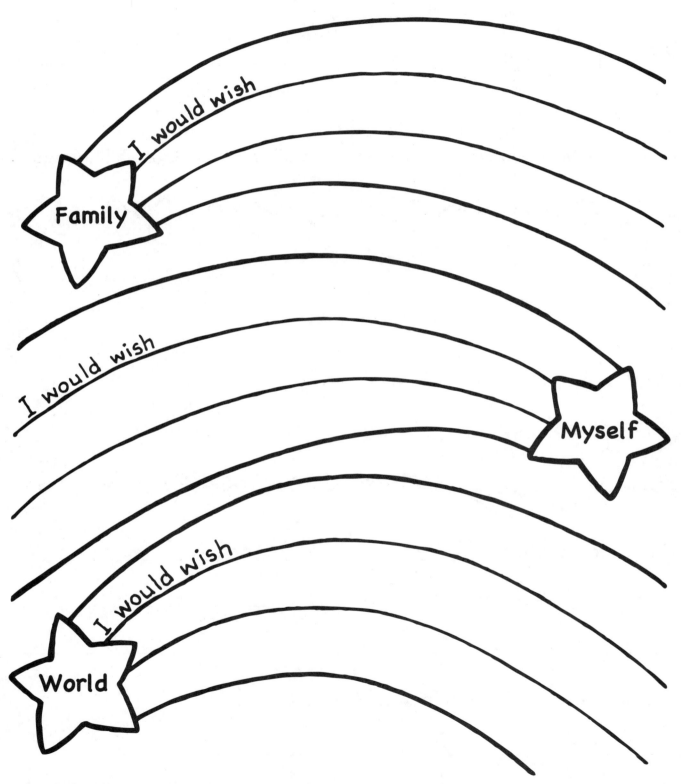